Basic Skills
Cause & Effect
Using Causes and Effects to Make Connections

Grades 5-6

by
Norm Sneller

Instructional Fair
An imprint of Carson-Dellosa Publishing LLC
Greensboro, North Carolina

Instructional Fair

Author: Norm Sneller
Project Director/Editor: Sara Bierling
Editors: Laura Bennett-Kimble, Susan Threatt
Cover Design: Matthew Van Zomeren
Cover Artist: Laura Zarrin
Interior Designer: Tracy L. Wesorick
Interior Artist: Mary Bucella

Instructional Fair
An imprint of Carson-Dellosa Publishing LLC
PO Box 35665
Greensboro, NC 27425 USA

ISBN 978-0-74240-101-3
217108091

About the Book

Cause and Effect for grades 5–6 has been designed to apply a cross-curricular approach to the practice of cause and effect skills. The book brings home to students the application of cause and effect skills through the content areas they study every day. Additionally, character skills are enhanced as students work through practical life applications to examine consequences of actions through critical thinking. Students of a wide range of abilities will find this book valuable. Activities are written to guide students carefully, yet challenge them to move forward based on personal ability.

Table of Contents

Name _____

U-Pick

Look at the pictures carefully. Circle the best answer to each question below.

1. Why does the dog bark?

   a. It smells food.

   b. It hears a prowler.

   c. It is ready for its nap.

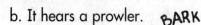

2. Why is Marti so happy?

   a. She's excited about tomorrow's race.

   b. She's going to the circus.

   c. She did well on a test.

3. Why is Henry wet?

   a. He fell into a pool.

   b. Maddie dumped water on his head.

   c. He recently took a shower.

4. Why is Mr. Pinski speeding?

   a. He loves to drive fast.

   b. He hopes to get to the theater on time.

   c. His wife is having a baby.

5. Why does Tasha scowl?

   a. She let a goal slip through.

   b. Her pet python is ill.

   c. Her friends are laughing at her.

6. Why can't Mrs. Collins sleep?

   a. Her husband is snoring.

   b. Her baby is crying.

   c. Her pillow is missing.

Try this: Create your own problem on the back of the page using one of these questions: Why does Goldilocks run away? Why is the sky blue? Why is José in trouble?

IF5628 • Cause & Effect 5-6

It's Great!

Look at the pictures carefully. Circle the best answer to each question below.

1. Why is the tiger imprisoned?

   a. It will be sent to a zoo.

   b. It has killed a farmer's goat.

   c. So it can be kept safe.

2. Why does Mr. Dilkins visit the zoo?

   a. His children beg him to take them.

   b. He loves monkeys.

   c. He is the zoo veterinarian.

3. Why does the tiger escape?

   a. It is hungry.

   b. It is running away from the zookeeper.

   c. It wanted some exercise.

4. Why is Mr. Dilkins running?

   a. He needs to catch a taxi.

   b. He's escaping a tiger.

   c. He's practicing for the Boston Marathon.

5. Why does the tiger stop chasing?

   a. He came to a stop sign.

   b. He is distracted by the video arcade.

   c. Mr. Dilkins escaped.

6. Why don't the players at the video arcade fear the tiger?

   a. The building door is locked.

   b. The tiger doesn't look scary.

   c. Zoo authorities come to the rescue.

What They Saw... What They Did

> Cut out the cause/effect strips and match them as pairs.
> Glue the pairs on the boxes on page 7 and then illustrate them.

a.

A small, frightened spaniel whimpered along the side of the busy highway.

d.

At school, the sixth grade class discussed the plight of families who had no food for their Thanksgiving meal.

b.

Carefully, Grandpa pulled off to the road's shoulder to let Grandma out to rescue the shivering creature.

e.

In the market, an anxious man frantically checked every one of his pockets and knelt in the aisle looking for his lost wallet.

c.

Dan and Joel stayed to search with him until it was discovered in the groceries of his shopping cart.

f.

The class raised money, purchased food, contacted a relief agency, got the name of a needy family, and delivered the meal.

Try this: Make your own sets of sentence strips and challenge a classmate to match them.

Name _____

What They Saw... What They Did (cont.)

1.
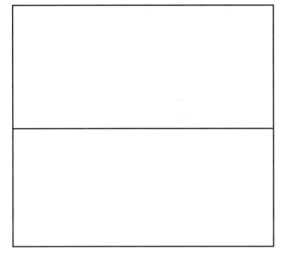

2.

3.
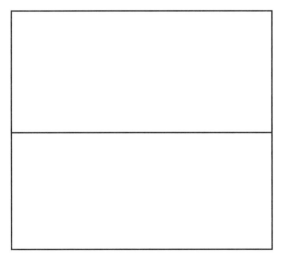

7

The Right Cause

Look at the four causes in large print. Find the effects on page 9 that match each of the causes and write them in the balloons.

Captain Colossal is the strongest human on Earth.

My sister is so kind!

Ben is sure he saw a UFO.

The Right Cause (cont.)

The tornado was heading straight for our town.

a. grabbed flashlight and blankets

b. has never been beaten in wrestling

c. looks up at the sky every night

d. punches holes in titanium with his fist

e. is afraid to look under the bed

f. volunteers to baby-sit for free

g. dashed to our cellar

h. called everyone together

i. can pick up Neanderthal Nate

j. no one believes a word he says

k. helps me with homework

l. all my friends love her

 9

Is It You, My Love?

Look at the sentence pairs below. Label the cause with a **C**. Label the effect with an **E**. Notice the letter guides below each sentence pair. Use these to fill in the blanks below.

1. ____ Juliet was bored silly.

   ____ On Friday afternoon, Juliet was at home alone.

   E = Y, C = S

2. ____ Romeo imagined Juliet as a vision of loveliness.

   ____ He strolled to her house to see his love.

   E = I, C = S

3. ____ Juliet was feeding her dog, Alfie.

   ____ Alfie wagged his tail vigorously.

   E = S, C = A

4. ____ Fearful of dogs, Romeo turned tail and ran.

   ____ Romeo spotted Alfie.

   E = T, C = E

5. ____ Alfie sighed as he went to his cage.

   ____ Romeo peered from behind a bush.

   E = P, C = I

6. ____ Juliet blushed.

   ____ Romeo stared lovingly at Juliet.

   E = O, C = R

7. ____ Juliet yawned with constraint.

   ____ Romeo chatted about his family's Buick LeSabre.

   E = L, C = R

8. ____ Romeo sang *I Love You Truly*.

   ____ Juliet covered her ears with her hands.

   E = T, C = I

9. ____ Romeo was crestfallen.

   ____ Juliet angrily told Romeo to leave.

   E = E, C = A

10. ____ Romeo planned to regain Juliet's heart.

    ____ Paris jealously hovered over Juliet.

    E = S, C = L

11. ____ Romeo called Paris a dithering dodo.

    ____ Paris gave Romeo a knuckle sandwich.

    E = S, C = H

12. ____ In a huff, Juliet left the combatants.

    ____ The fighters stopped to stare at the star-crossed lover.

    E = Y, C = T

13. ____ Juliet accepted Romeo's remorseful apology.

    ____ Romeo, on hands and knees, begged pardon of Juliet.

    E = T, C = E

14. ____ Romeo looked *w* up on his online dictionary when he returned home.

    ____ Juliet wrote a love sonnet for Romeo.

    E = W, C = D

7E 9C 4E 13C 6C 13E 11C 2E 10E 5E 10C 3C 12E 8C 11E

recreated as 14E 4C 2C 8E 3E 5C 14C 9E 1C 12C 6E 7C 1E .

Name _____

Boy Meets Reality

Look at the six titles below. Each is the effect (or result) of one of the sets of numbered causes. Write the correct title for each set.

Effects

Boy Called Conceited Creampuff by Sister

Boy Misses Football Practice

Boy Sees Movie

Boy Shops with Sister

Boy Goes to Beach

Boy Writes Excellent Research Article

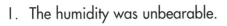

1. The humidity was unbearable.

   The summer sun shone fiercely.

   He was free to relax.   _____

2. He had no good clothes.

   He needed school supplies.

   He hoped to see friends at the mall.   _____

3. Everyone was talking about it.

   Dani offered to take him.

   He had just received his allowance.   _____

4. He couldn't find his books.

   He overslept again.

   He dawdled over breakfast.   _____

5. He showered for forty minutes.

   He played with his hair for ten minutes.

   He stood before the mirror for twenty minutes.   _____

6. He went to the media lab.

   He organized his notes.

   He followed the instructions faithfully.   _____

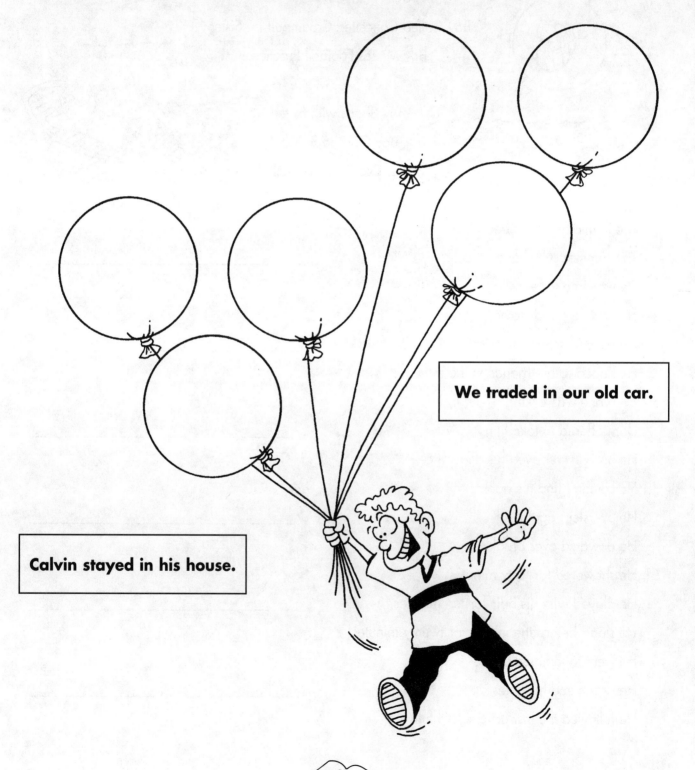

Name _____

Up and Away!

Look at the effects in bold print. Find the causes on page 13 that match each of the effects and write them inside the balloons.

We traded in our old car.

Calvin stayed in his house.

Up and Away! (cont.)

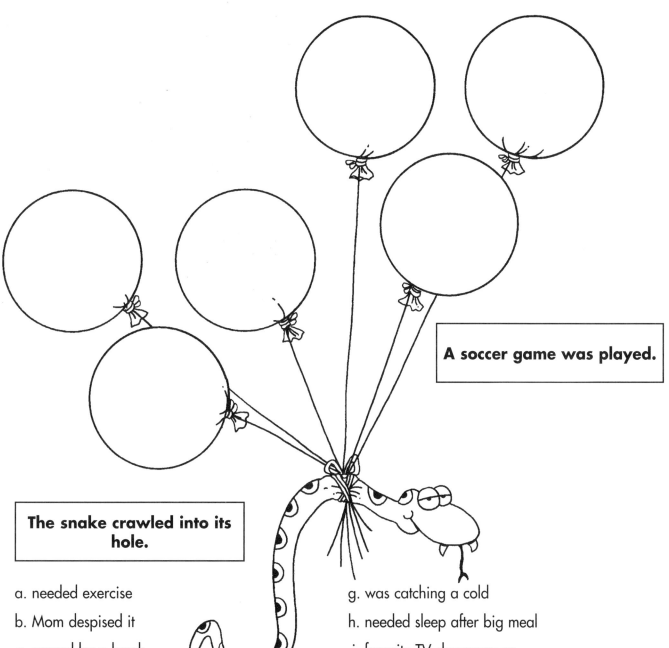

A soccer game was played.

The snake crawled into its hole.

a. needed exercise

b. Mom despised it

c. scared by a hawk

d. needed van to haul kids

e. it needed engine repair

f. love the game

g. was catching a cold

h. needed sleep after big meal

i. favorite TV show was on

j. air was turning chilly

k. beautiful, sunny day

l. had to tend young

Sweeter Than Honey

Look at the six titles below. Each is the effect (or result) of one of the sets of numbered causes. Write the correct title for each set.

Effects

"Evil" Bees Harmful to Large Colonies

Bee Colonies Complex, Say Scientists

Farmers Depend on Bees for Livelihood

Flowering Plants Vital to Bees

Bees Diverse Insects

1. Pollen is a protein source.

   Pollen is also a food source for bee larvae.

   Flower nectar is an energy source.

   _____

2. Bees are found in most world regions.

   Bees may be yellow, black, gray, blue, red, or green in color.

   Bees may range from 2mm to 4cm in length.

   _____

3. Semi-social bees live in colonies of two to seven.

   Each group consists of a queen and her daughter workers.

   Such colonies are temporary.

   _____

4. Some bees produce honey.

   Beeswax is harvested from honeycombs to sell.

   Bees provide pollination required for many fruits and vegetables.

   _____

5. A certain bee lays eggs in other colonies' cells.

   It will kill the resident queen.

   The bee forces the colony's workers to raise its parasitic young.

Now I Understand

Underline the cause phrase and circle the effect phrase in each sentence.

1. When Omar stubbed his toe, he cried out, "Yowsers!"

2. Tabitha was shocked when she saw her mother kissing Santa Claus under the mistletoe.

SMOOCH!

3. The rain was coming into the house, so we shut the windows.

4. Because I had eaten my mama's chicken soup, I slept like a baby.

5. Karen got very angry when she missed an easy lay-up.

6. The recording of the marvelous Madame Dilliere's masterpieces was so rich and clear that the glass in our classroom door shattered.

7. Our volcano erupted when we mixed vinegar and baking soda.

8. After it stumbled down the rough mountain trail, my horse became lame.

9. At the airport, David had an upset stomach because he was afraid of flying.

10. When the theater lights were turned on, I was blinded for a moment.

11. Because he is interested in modern art, Ted begged to see the newest art exhibit.

12. Tanya said, "Go fish!" because she had no kings.

Try this: Illustrate one of these sentences as if it were a photo in an album.

Caption Capers

Write the phrases from page 17 on the lines to match each picture with its cause or effect.

1.

_____
_____
_____

4.

_____
_____
_____

2.

_____
_____
_____
_____

5.

_____
_____
_____

3.

_____
_____
_____
_____

6.

_____
_____
_____
_____

Name _____

Caption Capers (cont.)

7.

_____
_____
_____
_____

9.

_____
_____
_____
_____

8.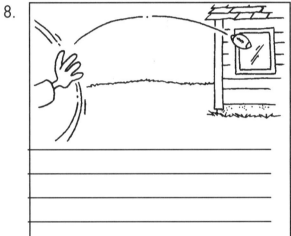

_____
_____
_____
_____

10.

_____
_____
_____
_____

Phrases

a. Tomás went to Mrs. Kater's front door to apologize.

b. Derek ran for his life.

c. To impress the girls at school…

d. Betsy was tired the next day.

e. Because the car ran out of gas…

f. Because Bart's sister takes long showers…

g. The fruit drink was nasty.

h. Classmates often go to Don for assistance.

i. Because an electrical storm rose up…

j. Because Marianne hit a home run…

Name _____

Traveling with the Corps

Underline the cause phrase and circle the effect phrase in each sentence.

1. When captured by the Hidasta tribe, Sacagawea, a Shoshone, was sold to a Mandan clan.

2. Chiefly because Jefferson was interested in finding a water route for trade to the Pacific Ocean, he commissioned an expedition called the Corps of Discovery.

3. Sacagawea joined the Corps of Discovery when her husband Toussaint Charbonneau was hired as a guide.

4. Because she was Shoshone, Sacagawea could help Lewis and Clark's expeditionary force obtain food and supplies from her people.

5. Sacagawea was also wanted for the trip as a token of peace, according to Clark.

6. As they began, she carried her son on her back because he was only a baby.

7. To move the expedition's freight up river, the group hired a large keelboat.

8. The boat nearly capsized but was rescued because of the young woman's quick thinking.

9. Due to her herbal knowledge, Sacagawea's tasks included gathering edible plants for the Corps.

10. The young woman was surprised when she met her older brother, now a chief among her people.

11. When a whale was beached along the Pacific Coast, Sacagawea begged and received permission to see the whale and the ocean up close.

12. Because her husband, and not she, was officially hired by the expedition, Sacagawea received no personal compensation for her work.

13. There are conflicting reports about Sacagawea's later life, so historians consider her a puzzle.

14. Clark became a Native-American agent as a result of his many encounters with native people.

15. When Sacagawea died in 1812, Clark adopted both of her children.

Name _____

Mystery Canyon

Cut on the solid outer lines of the brochure. Based on the information below, design a layout of Mystery Canyon on the back side of this page. Then complete the problems. Finally, fold the paper on the dotted lines to form a two-fold brochure.

Join us at Mystery Canyon and have the thrill of your life.

- **Descend** the Ladder of Terror, named for the accidental fall of Charles E. Glondin, a famous performer.

- **Hike** the cavern's many trails.

  a. **Starter**   .25 mi.
  b. **Easy**   1.5 mi.
  c. **Challenge** 4.7 mi.
  d. **Crazy fool** 6.2 mi.

- **Explore** the catacombs. Here, Blue Tooth's gang lay low for six weeks when the federal authorities discovered they were in Bone County.

- **Duck** while the Great Bats of Fluttering Chamber swoop overhead.

- **Dive** into the Witchings Broil. These are our own natural hot springs of medicinal waters. Temperatures range from 102–110° F (39–43° C). Towels provided. **No children under age 12.**

- **See** the Johnny Todd Exhibit. J. Todd explored the cavern in 1929. He was lost inside it for two years and lived on spring water and insects.

- **Relax** in Cubby Hole. This is our singularly novel one-person hole-in-the-wall for overnight lodging. TVs provided. Community wash stations.

Circle the correct answer.

1. You must duck your head in Fluttering Chamber because...

   a. it's so short.
   b. bats fly about.
   c. it's the law.

2. You may wish to bring a swimsuit because...

   a. water drips from overhead.
   b. the air is so hot.
   c. you can dive into the Witchings Broil.

3. Because J. Todd became lost in 1929...

   a. he missed World War II.
   b. he never saw an exhibit.
   c. he had to live on water and insects.

Visit

Mystery Canyon

For a uniquely tantalizing experience

Mystery Canyon, Inc.
P.O. Box 495
Bone County, IN
98765-4321
Credit cards accepted

© Carson-Dellosa

 19

IF5628 • Cause & Effect 5-6

Wilbur Lives!

Read the two editorials expressing different opinions regarding a particular animal pet. Then answer the questions.

Dear Editor,

I am shocked with the outcry against loving families who wish to have pigs for pets. How can people be so ignorant? Our little Sweet Blossom is a lovely little animal. Unlike dogs, which "do their thing" wherever they wish, Sweet Blossom will only go where we allow him. Pigs are so intelligent. They are much superior to cats and dogs. They are quickly able to perform new tricks, communicate with humans, and read our emotions. I wish that all people were as bright as my little sweetie! Furthermore, pigs are clean beasts. They wash themselves in water frequently. If clean water is available, a pig prefers it to mud, which, by the way, is a pig's method for keeping cool in the summer heat.

Emma Feinswein

Dear Editor,

Sure I like pigs! For brats, sausages, chops, and bacon. But as a pet? No way! Down on the farm, we know where pigs belong—in their sty. A pig no more belongs in a house than a bee in your bonnet. It's stupid to believe pigs even want to live indoors. It isn't natural. And pigs can be vicious. I've seen some terrible things. Pig violence against humans is not a pretty sight, let me assure you. Let's not throw pearls before swine. And for heaven's sake, we should do what's natural for the beast.

Eugene Barnhardt

Circle the correct answer.

1. Emma Feinswein thinks pigs are more intelligent than dogs and cats because…

   a. their brains have more wrinkles.

   b. pigs "read" our emotions.

   c. pigs don't make too much noise.

2. Eugene Barnhardt thinks that owning pigs as pets isn't natural because…

   a. pigs should be killed.

   b. pigs are meant to be eaten.

   c. a pig will make your spouse jealous.

3. Write **F** (Feinswein) or **B** (Barnhardt) to identify the source of each detail.

   ____ little sweetie   ____ clean beasts

   ____ what is natural   ____ bee in bonnet

   ____ Sweet Blossom   ____ pig violence

   ____ sausage   ____ keep cool

   ____ pearls before swine

Name _____

What Happened?

Look at the six sets of causes below. Write the effect you might expect from each.

1. The child stretched the balloon.
   He put it to his lips.
   He pursed his lips around the balloon's neck.

   _____

   _____

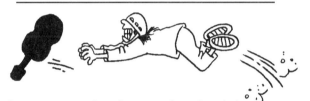

2. She was in such a hurry riding her bike.
   She carried her viola across the bars.
   She failed to see the rock on the street in front of her.

   _____

   _____

3. We had a tremendous snowstorm during the night.
   Winds gusted to 45 mph (72 km/h).
   The roads are blocked.

   _____

   _____

4. I ran as fast as I could.
   I passed all the other runners.
   I wasn't even tired.

   _____

   _____

5. I awoke and had my breakfast.
   I pulled out my toothbrush.
   I smeared ADA-approved paste over the bristles.

   _____

   _____

6. Dani held her burger in her hand, even though she had already eaten a large lunch.
   Her pup looked up at her with those begging eyes.
   Sighing, the dog rested its head on her lap.

   _____

   _____

IF5628 • Cause & Effect 5-6

Name _____

Squealing

(Read the story, then answer the questions on page 23.)

You know how it is with little kids. They tend to exaggerate so much you can't believe anything they say.

So, when Teralynn poked her head into my room the other day to tell me "all heck's breakin' loose" (Mom was out getting groceries so she dared say that), I figured a couple of chickens had gotten loose. So I just stayed in bed where I was doing my math homework for school.

"Danny! You'd better get your scrawny behind out here or Dad'll yell at you!"

Well, I jumped out of bed then. We don't naturally threaten about Dad's rantings unless we mean business.

The kids were all outside, so I stepped off the porch, letting the screen door slam behind me. I heard voices over by the barn, so I followed the screams and grunts of the pigs. *Oh, mercy!* The pigs were out again.

I dashed to the barn. All the way I could hear grunting, squealing, and hollering. It was so bad I couldn't tell the kids' sounds from the pigs'. I never even made it to the barn. Those pigs were running all over the yard. Davey and Missy were flying after them like they were kamikazes or something. Teralynn just stood there with her fists clenched, screaming orders to the younger kids. The pigs were smarter and faster than those kids. They dashed this way and that. There was no way we could catch them. If a pig doesn't want to be

caught, forget it.

We thought we'd walk a line side by side and push them back in through the barn door. No matter how we tried it, those pigs sneaked between us.

"Teralynn," I yelled, "you fix the gate so they can't escape again. Missy and Davey, you grab those poles by the shed and stand back out of the way by the fence. If those critters come your way, you scare 'em back."

I decided to let out Bonnie Belle. Bonnie's a big, shiny black mare. She doesn't like those pigs, and they don't trust her. Bonnie Belle is fast and tricky and can dodge as good as any of them.

I let Bonnie out of the barn, and she saw those pork bellies. She just flared her nostrils, pricked up her ears, let out a whinny, and started galloping wild circles around the yard.

The pigs squealed like banshees set afire. They high-tailed it away from her back into the barn and into their pen again. It didn't take more than three minutes total. Missy and Teralynn shut the pen up and that was that.

I took Bonnie by her harness. "That's it, girl. You did a good job," I said, and I fed her two cubes of sugar.

Name _____

Squealing (cont.)

Complete the following sentences.

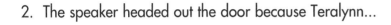

1. Teralynn thought she could get away with bad language because...

_____

_____

2. The speaker headed out the door because Teralynn...

_____

_____

3. The speaker headed toward the barn because...

_____

_____

4. When he heard grunts, the speaker knew...

_____

_____

5. Because the pigs were smarter than those kids...

_____

_____

6. Bonnie Belle started galloping wild circles around the yard when...

_____

_____

An Unfinished Journal

Look at the six sets of causes below. Write the effect you might expect from each.

1. Mom needed fuel for the cooking stove.
   Dad needed wood for the fireplace.
   I wasn't doing anything.

   _____

   _____

2. Our milk cow mooed mournfully.
   Dad had gone to town on business.
   Mom was caring for the other kids.

   _____

   _____

3. Corn was growing knee high.
   Weeds were growing nicely, too.
   I wasn't doing anything.

   _____

   _____

4. Locusts swarmed over our fields like brown clouds.
   Nothing could convince them to leave.
   We set smoky fires to drive them off.

   _____

   _____

5. Crows love corn.
   The corn was ripening fast.
   Mom gave me some straw and some old clothes.

   _____

   _____

6. The cabin was too dark for reading.
   I couldn't light a fire in the hearth in the hot weather.
   A lantern sat on the table.

   _____

   _____

Good Manners Yuck!

Read the editorial. Then answer the questions below.

Dear Editor,

We should instruct all members of our society in proper manners. I know that many folks write in this forum to decry the poor manners of young people. I dare say the problem lies with adults as much as with children. Here are three manner deficiencies that affect many.

People should refrain from spitting in public. It is disgusting to those who are unwilling (and unwitting) spectators. It puts self over society. I am convinced that people who spit openly have little or no awareness of other people. It is an unsanitary practice. The germs are a vicious predator, waiting for hands and feet to fall prey to their power.

Pedestrians should know the importance of "stepping to the right." I often take walks. I cannot begin to tell you how often I must step off the sidewalk (even into the street!) to avoid being knocked over by approaching walkers. I am a 72-year-old woman and find it hard to get up off the ground when I fall. When people walk together, they may walk side-by-side. But when they meet another pedestrian, they should step to the right and walk in single file. It's just that simple.

Finally, too often adults loudly threaten and punish their children in public. I loathe public displays of discipline. Sometimes I wonder if such parents are merely showing off their power. As if I'm impressed! If one must confront one's child for misbehavior, a quiet voice should suffice, I think. Speaking harshly and loudly to an active, emotional child is asking for trouble. It reinforces the behavior of the child. Remember that a gentle answer turns away wrath.

Sincerely,
Mrs. Edith Seemingly

1. Label the effects with the causes that produce them.

A People spit openly   **B** People walk thoughtlessly   **C** People address children harshly

_____ knock over others   _____ others become disgusted   _____ selfish

_____ reinforces bad behavior   _____ forced to step aside

_____ asking for trouble   _____ unsanitary

2. Do you agree or disagree with the writer? Why?

_____

3. What manner(s) would you add to this editorial?

_____

4. Argue for or against: Adults need manners training as much as children.

_____

Name _____

WHRT—The Radio Station with Heart

Hillary becomes so emotional when she tunes in to WHRT's programs.
Imagine what effect is produced on Hillary as she listens to the
following segments. Write the appropriate effect on the line. Use each emotion once.

1. On Hillary's favorite radio soap, Dusty Dreamkiss falls into her second coma in six weeks.

   _____

2. Bob Bubblejet, host of *Hats off to Laughter*, shares a hysterical anecdote.

   _____

3. Roberta Snack, the newest star of the millennium, croons a song of romance.

   _____

4. An audio version of the hip-hugging ad for New Army Jeans stirs Hillary's emotions.

   _____

5. News: *All area schools will have three additional days in June due to finance reform.*

   _____

6. Sports Beat: *The girls' high school basketball team has won the state championship.*

   _____

7. Daphne Deltoid has completed her fifteen-minute *Aerobics on the Air* program.

   _____

8. News: *War has broken out in the rolling hills of Svedelheim today.*

   _____

9. The station manager announces a new clue for *Mystery Prize*.

   _____

10. News: *The child reported missing this morning has been found. He is safe.*

   _____

Emotional Effects

angry	convinced	elated	giggly
relieved	speculative	swooning	weepy
wiped out	worried		

Name _____

On the Job

Ariel Speaks is press secretary to Mayor Bonnie Last, of New Horizons, Connecticut. Here is her schedule for April 14.

6:00	walk the dog
6:30	shower and breakfast
7:00	train commute to office
8:30	arrive/check messages
9:00	meet with Team 1
10:00	tour recycling plant
11:00	interview the plant's supervisor
12:00	lunch meeting with Mayor Last
12:45	call Kyle's school re: progress report

1:00	meet with Team 2
2:00	take care of correspondence
3:00	conference call with city council members re: recycling plans
4:00	formulate press release re: mayor's position on city-wide recycling
5:00	train commute home
6:30	grab food from deli for supper

Circle the most reasonable response.

1. Because the plant supervisor called in sick,...

    a. Ariel couldn't meet with the mayor.

    b. Ariel was sent to Alberta.

    c. Ariel had a longer lunch break.

2. Because Kyle's teacher spoke for twenty minutes,...

    a. Ariel didn't hear about her son's work.

    b. Ariel was late for a team meeting.

    c. Ariel missed lunch.

3. Because the train had a twenty-minute delay in the morning,...

    a. Ariel had no breakfast.

    b. Ariel couldn't check her messages.

    c. Ariel missed her meeting with Team 1.

4. Because Team 2 needed ninety minutes to go over problems,...

    a. Ariel had less time for correspondence.

    b. Ariel decided to call Kyle's school back.

    c. Ariel noticed cracks in the office walls.

5. How long is Ariel's commute one way?

    _____

    _____

6. State two questions Ariel might ask at the recycling plant.

    _____

    _____

7. If Mayor Last decides to go ahead with free city recycling, what argument might be used against such plans?

    _____

    _____

27

IF5628 • Cause & Effect 5-6

Camp Letter

Read the letter Sasha sent to her friend Jen from camp. Then complete the activity on page 29.

Dear Jen,

Camp so far has been great! I'm in a cabin with seven other girls and a camp counselor. Her name is Maya, and she's very cool. She lets us read after lights out, and she tells the best ghost stories ever.

Tasha is a really nice girl who's in my cabin. She's also on Red Team with me. We were partners for the wall climb. That's one of our partnership challenges. We had to help each other climb up a bare wall with no steps or anything. It was hard work, but it was a lot of fun. We also had to build a cabin together using only natural materials. Our whole team had fun with that one. I'm hoping Tasha will be my partner for the trust fall we're doing tomorrow.

The food here is actually pretty good. Last night some of the counselors cooked dinner for us on the campfire. They made hot dogs and corn on the cob. It was great!

I miss all the kids back home on Russell Street, though. No one here wants to play Hearts with me. A lot of the girls only want to talk about what the boys are doing. And it's too bad Mr. Torres can't drive his ice-cream cart all the way out here to Gull Lake. I could really use a lime sherbet cone right now.

Well, I'll see you at the end of the week. Give Squirts a hug for me.

Sasha

Camp Letter (cont.)

1. Explain three things that cause Sasha to like being at camp.

_____

_____

_____

_____

_____

_____

2. Explain three things that cause Sasha to miss being at home.

_____

_____

_____

_____

_____

_____

3. Explain why you think the campers were completing the challenges mentioned in paragraph two of Sasha's letter.

_____

_____

_____

_____

_____

_____

Try this: Plan your own summer camp. Pick names for cabins or teams. Create interesting team building games. Plan a calendar of events for a week at summer camp.

Long Ago

(Connect each cause with its matching effect.)

Cause

____ 1. The Princess kisses the frog.

____ 2. There was a pea under the mattress.

____ 3. Rapunzel was kept secluded in a high tower.

____ 4. The Beast is kind to Beauty.

____ 5. The fairy was not invited to Aurora's christening.

____ 6. Jack cut down the beanstalk.

____ 7. Cinderella's foot fit into the glass slipper easily.

____ 8. Snow White ate the apple.

____ 9. Grandmother was ill.

____ 10. Hansel showed a thin bone to the witch.

____ 11. The youngster's porridge was gone.

____ 12. The third pig built his house out of bricks.

Effect

a. She thought he was still too skinny.

b. The handsome prince married his lady.

c. She agrees to marry him.

d. The wolf could not blow the house down.

e. She fell into a death-like sleep.

f. Baby Bear wailed.

g. She cast a hateful spell on the child.

h. Red Ridinghood brought her cookies.

i. The giant fell to the ground.

j. The princess could not sleep.

k. He regains his human form.

l. She had never met any men before.

Name _____

One Day in the Life Buzz! 6:00

Evan Denison is a busy sixth-grade kid. Fill in his day's schedule for a Saturday last fall.

6:00	_____
6:30	_____
6:35	_____
7:30	_____
8:00	_____
10:30	_____
11:30	_____
12:00	_____
2:30	_____
3:30	_____
6:00	_____
8:00	_____
9:00	_____
10:30	_____

Here are your clues:

1. Because Evan had lunch before noon and then shopped for 2.5 hours...

2. Because the 55-minute paper route immediately preceded breakfast...

3. Because he postponed homework as long as possible...

4. Because he baby-sat for 2.5 hours...

5. Because these three events occurred in order: baby-sat, picnic, and TV wrestling...

6. Because he did chores for one hour in the afternoon...

7. Because he rested after his football game by playing a new video game...

Events

picnic supper	homework
baby-sit	football game
shop for clothes	breakfast
shower and sleep	paper route
new video game	alarm wakes up
lunch	chores
watch wrestling on TV	
alarm wakes up again	

Name _____

Around the World

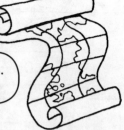

Below are facts about Ferdinand Magellan's famous explorations. Connect each cause with its matching effect.

Cause

_____ 1. Trading would make investors rich.

_____ 2. The Portuguese controlled the sea route to the East Indies.

_____ 3. Seamen prepared to ward off enemies.

_____ 4. The crew's food supplies ran out.

_____ 5. The Spanish ships had a long journey across the Pacific.

_____ 6. Magellan's own men were loyal to him.

_____ 7. The mapmakers had underestimated the size of the Pacific Ocean.

_____ 8. Magellan offered to help an island ruler warring with another.

_____ 9. The shores the ships passed were illuminated by the fires of the natives.

_____ 10. The Portuguese controlled the African Cape of Good Hope.

_____ 11. The *Victoria* was caught in a vicious storm.

_____ 12. The surviving ships took on a cargo of cloves.

Effect

a. Spanish explorers dared not travel sout around Africa.

b. The ship returned to Spain with its sails in tatters.

c. Ships were sent to the Far East to trade.

d. Magellan was killed in the conflict.

e. Magellan was able to squelch a mutiny by some of the crew.

f. They were forced to eat sawdust, leather sail rigging, and rats.

g. Magellan named this land *Tierra del Fuego* (land of fire).

h. Seamen suffered from thirst, malnutrition, and starvation while crossing the ocean.

i. The Spanish hoped to discover a different route to the Spice Islands by traveling west.

j. Food and water supplies were quickly used up.

k. Despite the loss of ships, the voyage earned a profit.

l. The ships were armed with guns and cannons.

Name _____

Can You Tell?

Look at the sentence pairs below. Label the cause with a **C**. Label the effect with an **E**.

1. ____Dogs bark at noises.

   ____Many people own them to protect their properties.

2. ____We call ants social insects.

   ____They live in colonies.

Whoops!

3. ____Newspapers can sell for reduced prices.

   ____Newspapers contain many advertisements.

4. ____Cats are extremely agile creatures.

   ____When dropped, cats land on their feet.

5. ____Few mammals can care for themselves at birth.

   ____Most mammals are born immature.

6. ____The sun has a powerful gravitational force.

   ____The earth revolves around the sun.

7. ____Banana growing requires a tropical climate.

   ____Bananas are not grown in Maine.

8. ____People fear snakes.

   ____Snakes are described as evil creatures in many stories.

9. ____People must take precautions against skin cancer.

   ____The ozone layer is thinning.

10. ____Many humans fear what they do not know.

    ____They tend to prejudge that which is different.

11. ____Most television and radio commercials include music.

    ____Music helps recall our memories.

12. ____Young children view more violent television than their parents did.

    ____Children may exhibit tendencies to act more violently.

IF5628 • Cause & Effect 5-6

Name _____

Let's Get Lyrical

Lyle Lipscomb, the prolific writer of the 1960s and '70s, has written lyrics for country and western stars such as P.B. Sandwich, Sherry Lou, and Nan Tuckett. Sad to say, he has come on hard times in recent years. He is presently working as a used car salesman in Waco, Texas. Below are a few of his recent, and as yet unrecorded, songs. Match the first line of each song with the second. Place the numbers on the blanks provided. The last words of the first lines will give you clues.

1. You May Call Me Sweetie Pie
2. For You I'll Always Pine
3. Remember When We Wuz Towed
4. If You Come up from Savannah
5. Because Your Eyes Are Brown
6. When We Strolled in the Moonlight
7. My Horse, I Call Her Piggy,
8. Since You Woke Me from That Dream
9. My Legs They Turned into Apricot Jelly
10. Since You Pointed at My Tummy
11. Oh Lord, My Fingers Can No Longer Snap
12. Oh, If You'll Have Me Play Your Hand
13. Please Don't Give Me the Shoe

_____ I Will Never Leave This Town
_____ I've Been Feeling Pretty Crummy
_____ You Got That Huge Mosquito Bite
_____ 'Cuz a Frog Got into the Radiator?
_____ Ever Since My Honey Said, "Shut Your Trap"
_____ If You Needle Me No More
_____ I've Been Living Nightmares
_____ I'll Buy You a Piano Grand
_____ 'Cuz You're My Lemon Custard
_____ Since She Scarfed Down All My Food
_____ And I'll Be Your Heel Forever
_____ When You Ordered Toast and Jam
_____ I Will Be Your Top Banana

IF5628 • Cause & Effect 5-6

Have I Got a Job for You

> Read the five job opportunities below. Match each job applicant
> with a job or jobs below by writing the correct numbers on each line.

1. **Bakers Wanted**. Must know flour from powdered sugar. Ability to read is required. Must be 18 years or older. Call Bun in the Oven at 267-1010. Ask for Rose.

2. **Yard Work**. Like to work up a sweat? Eager to work with loud machines? We've got many positions for hardworking men. Call Hulk at 268-8760.

3. **Candy Sales**. Sugar-N-Spice is looking for door-to-door sales reps willing to work strictly on commission. Must be at least 16 years old. $100 deposit on first order of candy. Call 1-800-GOCANDY.

4. **Child Care**. Looking for a 12- to 16-year-old girl to care for my precious 3-year-old. Must love children and ferrets. Need for evening care. Call Mommy at 264-9800.

5. **Photogenic?** We need students ages 7–14 to model for our Fall Series Clothing Sale. Must have no police record. For the required parental permission form write: P.O. Box 9009, Good Pose, IA 50014.

_____ Tad: 14-year-old boy; has no money

_____ Blanche: 16-year-old girl; hates noise

_____ Anselm: 19-year-old man; cannot read

_____ Zoe: 18-year-old woman; won't work door-to-door

_____ Perry: 17-year-old female; doesn't know baking ingredients

Try this: Each applicant found a different job from those on this list. What job did each find?

A Midsummer's Day Cream

Read the play synopsis below. Then answer the cause and effect questions.

Cast

Argus—a young lord

Benvolio—Argus's squire

Clarissa—a quick-minded female

Desdemona—Clarissa's maid

Eureka—a scholarly maid

Fozzy—a scruffy buffoon

Synopsis: A young lord and his squire are returning home from the wars. Coming into a Greek village, they are confronted by the beauteous Clarissa, a quick-minded female of singular purpose—marriage. She and her maid, Desdemona, lay traps to capture the hearts of the two warriors. In a secondary plot, a scholarly maid is comically courted by a scruffy buffoon whose first love is honey.

Act One   the forest

Act Three   the churchyard

Act Two   the marketplace

Act Four   the forest

Questions:

1. Why are two men walking through this town?

   a. They are returning from a war.

   b. They are lost.

   c. Their horses have run off.

2. The two soldiers should be on guard because...

   a. the Greeks are their enemies.

   b. a buffoon loves honey.

   c. two ladies wish to capture their hearts.

3. We know the events of this play occur in a twenty-four–hour time period because...

   a. the story is short.

   b. the title declares it.

   c. the synopsis explains it.

Try this: Create one of the following:

- an opening line for Argus

- a food-related four-line song for Fozzy

- a short conversation between Clarissa and Desdemona

Name _____

Pandas

Read the article. Then match the cause and effect statements by drawing a line.

The giant panda is an Asian mammal that lives on the mountain slopes of China. Pandas eat only bamboo, which grows extensively in the Chinese highlands. In order to get enough nutrients, a panda must eat as much as 85 pounds (39 kg) of bamboo a day. The rampant destruction of the panda's habitat has endangered this creature. The government of China has tried to save the panda's food supply by setting up reserves of bamboo-rich land. Large reserves are necessary to ensure adequate food for the pandas. Because bamboo plants take so long to grow into mature plants, there have been shortages in the past. These periodic shortages have led to the deaths of hundreds of pandas. Only about 1,000 giant pandas remain in the wild.

Cause

1. Many pandas die each year.

2. Pandas must get enough nutrients.

3. Bamboo takes a long time to mature.

4. There is rampant destruction of the panda habitat.

5. There have been bamboo shortages.

Effect

a. Pandas are endangered.

b. Hundreds of pandas have died.

c. They must eat huge amounts of bamboo.

d. Periodic bamboo shortages occur.

e. China has set up bamboo reserves.

Ancient Farming

Read the article. Then answer the questions on page 39.

Three ancient civilizations from the Americas were the Incan, the Aztec, and the Mayan. The Maya thrived in the area we now know as Mexico's Yucatan peninsula and Central America. The Incan Empire was located along the west coast of South America in what are known today as Peru and Chile. The Aztec lived in the area we know today as Mexico. Their capital city was in the same place as modern-day Mexico City. Agriculture was very important to all of these civilizations.

For the Aztecs, the common agricultural tool was a pointed stick used for digging. In areas covered with dense forest, farmers practiced slash-and-burn agriculture, in which they burned a section of forest and planted in the cleared areas. In this way, the ashes from the burn produced highly fertile soil. In hilly or mountainous regions, the farmers cut terraces into the hills to increase the amount of flat farmland on which to plant. Farmers also built island-gardens, called chinampas. They scooped up mud from lake bottoms and made islands that were suitable for planting. The chinampas yielded huge crops.

The Inca used a variety of farming methods. Along the coastal desert, they built networks to help irrigate the land. In mountainous areas, they cut terraces into the hillsides as the Aztecs did. Their farm fields were divided into three groups. One field was dedicated to the needs of local people. The other two supported state and religious activities.

Mayan farmers built raised fields similar to the chinampas of the Aztecs. They used swampy lowlands and drained the soil to unearth fields on which to grow their crops. They combined this technique with terracing to provide food to feed large populations.

Ancient Farming (cont.)

1. Why do you think agriculture may have been so important to these ancient civilizations?

_____

_____

_____

2. Why did slash-and-burn agriculture produce highly fertile soil?

_____

_____

_____

3. Why do you think the chinampa farms of the Aztecs yielded large crops?

_____

_____

_____

4. List one other reason why terracing might have been helpful to these ancient civilizations.

_____

_____

_____

5. The farming techniques of all three civilizations are similar even though the people lived in different areas. List two reasons why this might be.

_____

_____

_____

_____

_____

Sell It!

Look at the advertisement. Then answer the questions below.

1. Why do you think the advertisers picture a well-dressed couple in this ad?

   _____

   _____

   _____

2. Circle the values below that this ad brings to mind.

   a. wealth

   b. hard work

   c. marriage

   d. the simple life

3. Why would you want to buy this soda?

   _____

   _____

   _____

The Dust Bowl

(Read the following story. Then answer the questions below.)

A long time ago, many states in the mid- and southwest were covered with thick grass. Grass covered the land as far as the eye could see. This land was called the grassland.

Many settlers moved into the grasslands. They used the grassy fields to graze livestock like cows and sheep. Some settlers plowed the fields and planted wheat. However, these settlers used up the land so much that it became barren.

Then a six-year-long drought occurred. Little rain fell, and the sun scorched the settlers' crops. Because there was no more grass, the soil became loose. Strong winds caused the soil to form dust storms, covering buildings and roads with dusty soil. Soon, even the air became clogged with dust, and the people in these regions could not breathe. People began to call this region the "Dust Bowl." Things got so bad that many farmers were forced to move away.

Farmers in this region had to learn how to take care of the land. They planted trees to break the strong winds off the grasslands. They also planted crops in strips that followed the contours of the land. The strips created ridges that trapped rainwater and allowed it to soak into the land. The farmers learned from their mistakes and worked with the land to overcome the hardships of the Dust Bowl.

1. What caused the Dust Bowl?

_____

2. Why did the settlers move away from the Dust Bowl?

_____

3. Why did farmers plant trees?

_____

4. Why does planting crops in strips help the crops?

_____

5. What do you think is an important lesson to be learned from this story?

_____

Today's News

> Read the articles below. Then answer the questions on page 43.

Terrible Tornado Torments

A torrential tornado struck Toon Town yesterday causing a citywide power outage. When the 200-mile-per-hour (320 km/h) winds sped through the town, light poles, gazebos, and doghouses were blown down. The Tiny Toon electrical dam malfunctioned and sent the waters of Toon River rushing over Toonie Bridge. As a result, traffic on Toon Boulevard was backed up to Toon Place in the center of town. Because of the wide extent of the damage, officials estimate the cost of the clean-up will exceed $4 million.

Looters Rummage through Toon Town

Toon Town police have reported an increasing number of looting incidents since the tornado. Buildings damaged by the storm have been the prime target of teenage hoodlums out to do no good. Because of a broken front window, McDuck's Department Store has been relieved of all its display dummies. Several pricing placards were also stolen.

Boop's Drugstore has reported a surprisingly large number of ice-cream bar thefts. Apparently the gusting winds of the tornado ripped the door off their deep freezer. Due, presumably, to the power outage, Fudd's Hardware has lost a large supply of flashlights and kerosene lamps. Anyone with information regarding these thefts should contact the Toon Boulevard Police Precinct.

Town Picnic Postponed

As a result of yesterday's horrific natural disaster, the Toon Town Picnic has been postponed indefinitely. The mayor's office is reluctant to set a new date until the amount of damage and the reconstruction timetable have been assessed.

The picnic-planning meeting has also been cancelled until further notice. Committee members will be notified of its rescheduling. Anyone with concerns or inquiries should contact Daisy in the mayor's office.

Name _____

Today's News (cont.)

Write two cause and effect statements about each article on page 42.

1. Terrible Tornado Torments

_____
_____
_____

_____
_____

2. Looters Rummage through Toon Town

_____
_____
_____
_____
_____

3. Town Picnic Postponed

_____
_____
_____
_____
_____

Try this: Write your own newspaper article. Make sure you include plenty of causes and effects.

A Native Tale

Read Nina's book report below. Then answer the cause and effect questions on page 45.

Julie of the Wolves

by Jean Craighead George

Miyax, a thirteen-year-old native girl, grows up with her father in a seal-fishing village in Alaska. He teaches her all the old ways, like cleaning hides, making sleds out of frozen leather, and catching wild game to eat. When Miyax's relatives find out she isn't in school, they take her away from her father to a town where the old ways do not fit in. Miyax slowly learns English and attends a school where she can learn many new things about the modern world. In her new home, her friends have gussak, or white, names, so Miyax is called Julie. She starts to forget the old ways that her father taught her. She begins a penpal relationship with a girl in San Francisco and longs to go there so she can experience television and other modern conveniences.

Then Julie is whisked off into a marriage of convenience to a young boy her age. Though only a marriage in name, Julie is made to work for the boy's mother, sewing coats and boots for the gussak tourists. Finally, driven by the meanness of her "husband," Julie runs away, hoping to reach San Francisco and her penpal. Her father, she has heard, never returned home from a seal-fishing trip.

Soon Miyax (Julie) becomes lost on the Alaskan tundra with no food and only a sod hut for shelter. She makes her camp near a wolf den and befriends the pack, learning to speak their body language and becoming one of their family. Her new foster father is Amaroq, the majestic leader of the pack, who welcomes Miyax and helps to protect her.

When Miyax's new family decides it is time to migrate for the winter, Miyax travels with them, always just a few steps behind their pace. When the pack stops by a lake, Miyax stops too, only to be attacked by a bear. The next morning, Amaroq is shot by hunters from an airplane. The wolf pack is helpless without its leader and begins to forage for food. One of the wolf pups, Kapu, must take his place as the leader of the pack and eventually leads the pack on the hunt. When Miyax realizes her new family is all right, she decides to head off on her own.

While camped inside a newly made igloo, Miyax meets some of her people who tell her of their village and its leader, who Miyax realizes is the father she thought was dead. Miyax goes to the village but is disappointed that her father has given up many of the old ways and now embraces technology and the greedy ways of the gussak. Sadly, Miyax returns to the wild, determined to live by the old ways.

A Native Tale (cont.)

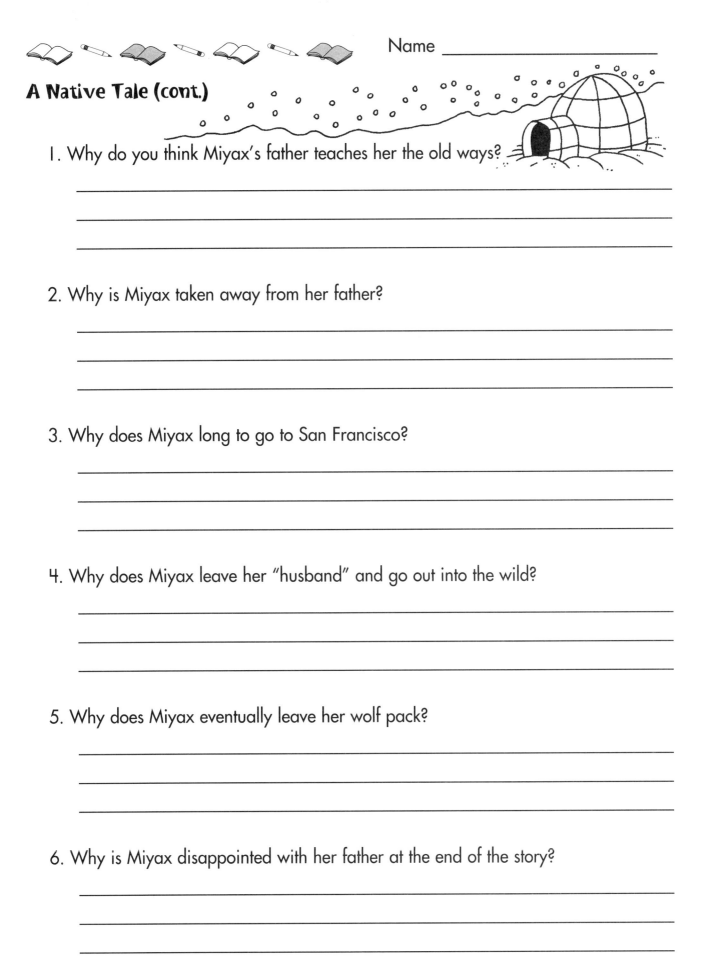

1. Why do you think Miyax's father teaches her the old ways?

_____

_____

_____

2. Why is Miyax taken away from her father?

_____

_____

_____

3. Why does Miyax long to go to San Francisco?

_____

_____

_____

4. Why does Miyax leave her "husband" and go out into the wild?

_____

_____

_____

5. Why does Miyax eventually leave her wolf pack?

_____

_____

_____

6. Why is Miyax disappointed with her father at the end of the story?

_____

_____

_____

Answer Key

1. a   4. a
2. c   5. a
3. b   6. a

1. a   4. b
2. b   5. b
3. a   6. c

a, b
c, e
d, f

Captain Colossal: b, d, i
my sister: f, k, l
Ben: c, e, j
tornado: a, g, h

1. E, C   8. C, E
2. C, E   9. E, C
3. C, E   10. C, E
4. E, C   11. C, E
5. C, E   12. C, E
6. E, C   13. E, C
7. E, C   14. E, C

Later this play is recreated as West Side Story.

1. Boy Goes to Beach
2. Boy Shops with Sister
3. Boy Sees Movie
4. Boy Misses Football Practice
5. Boy Called Conceited Creampuff by Sister
6. Boy Writes Excellent Research Article

car: b, d, e
Calvin: g, i, j

snake: c, h, l
soccer: a, f, k

1. Flowering Plants Vital to Bees
2. Bees Diverse Insects
3. Bee Colonies Complex, Say Scientists
4. Farmers Depend on Bees for Livelihood
5. "Evil" Bees Harmful to Large Colonies

1. **cause:** When Omar stubbed his toe,
   effect: he cried out, "Yowsers!"
2. **cause:** when she saw her mother kissing Santa Claus under the mistletoe.
   effect: Tabitha was shocked
3. **cause:** The rain was coming into the house,
   effect: so we shut the windows.
4. **cause:** Because I had eaten my mama's chicken soup,
   effect: I slept like a baby.
5. **cause:** when she missed an easy lay-up.
   effect: Karen got very angry
6. **cause:** The recording of the marvelous Madame Dilliere's masterpieces was so rich and clear that
   effect: the glass in our classroom door shattered.
7. **cause:** when we mixed vinegar and baking soda.
   effect: Our volcano erupted
8. **cause:** After it stumbled down the rough mountain trail,

effect: my horse became lame.
9. **cause:** because he was afraid of flying.
   effect: At the airport, David had an upset stomach
10. **cause:** When the theater lights were turned on,
    effect: I was blinded for a moment.
11. **cause:** Because he is interested in modern art,
    effect: Ted begged to see the newest art exhibit.
12. **cause:** because she had no kings.
    effect: Tanya said, "Go fish!"

1. e   2. i
3. j   4. c
5. f   6. d
7. b   8. a
9. g   10. h

1. **cause:** When captured by the Hidasta tribe,
   effect: Sacagawea, a Shoshone, was sold to a Mandan clan.
2. **cause:** Chiefly because Jefferson was interested in finding a water route for trade to the Pacific Ocean,
   effect: he commissioned an expedition called the Corps of Discovery.
3. **cause:** when her husband Toussaint Charbonneau was hired as a guide.
   effect: Sacagawea joined the

Corps of Discovery

4. **cause:** Because she was Shoshone,

   effect: Sacagawea could help Lewis and Clark's expeditionary force obtain food and supplies from her people.

5. **cause:** as a token of peace, according to Clark.

   effect: Sacagawea was also wanted for the trip

6. **cause:** because he was only a baby.

   effect: As they began, she carried her son on her back

7. **cause:** To move the expedition's freight up river,

   effect: the group hired a large keelboat.

8. **cause:** because of the young woman's quick thinking.

   effect: The boat nearly capsized but was rescued

9. **cause:** Due to her herbal knowledge,

   effect: Sacagawea's tasks included gathering edible plants for the Corps.

10. **cause:** when she met her older brother, now chief among her people.

    effect: The young woman was surprised

11. **cause:** When a whale was beached along the Pacific Coast,

    effect: Sacagawea begged and received permission to see it up close.

12. **cause:** Because her husband, and not she, was officially hired

by the expedition,

   effect: Sacagawea received no personal compensation for her work.

13. **cause:** There are conflicting reports about Sacagawea's later life,

   effect: so historians consider her a puzzle.

14. **cause:** as a result of his many encounters with the native people.

   effect: Clark became a Native-American agent

15. **cause:** When Sacagawea died in 1812,

   effect: Clark adopted both of her children.

1. b   2. c
3. c

1. b   2. b
3. F: little sweetie, Sweet Blossom, clean beasts, keep cool

   B: what is natural, sausage, pearls before swine, bee in bonnet, pig violence

1. The child blew up the balloon.
2. She hit the rock and fell off her bike.
3. School was cancelled.
4. I won the race.
5. I brushed my teeth.
6. Dani gave the dog some of her burger.

1. Mom was not there.
2. threatened that Dad would yell at him.

3. he heard voices by the barn.
4. that the pigs had gotten out again.
5. they couldn't be caught.
6. she saw the pigs.

1. I chopped some wood.
2. I milked the cow.
3. I weeded the garden.
4. The locusts left.
5. I made a scarecrow.
6. I read by the light of the lantern.

1. **A:** others become disgusted, unsanitary, selfish

   B: knock over others, forced to step aside

   C: reinforces bad behavior, asking for trouble

2. Answers will vary.
3. Answers will vary.
4. Answers will vary.

1. weepy   2. giggly
3. swooning   4. convinced
5. angry   6. elated
7. wiped out   8. worried
9. speculative   10. relieved

1. c   2. b
3. b   4. a
5. one and a half hours
6. Answers will vary.
7. Answers will vary.

1. nice camp counselor, met new friend, fun games, food is good
2. no one will play Hearts, only want to talk about boys, no lime sherbet

3. Answers will vary.

Long Ago 30

I. k	2. j
3. l	4. c
5. g	6. i
7. b	8. e
9. h	10. a
11. f	12. d

One Day in the Life 31

6:00—alarm wakes up

6:30—alarm wakes up again

6:35—paper route

7:30—breakfast

8:00—football game

10:30—new video game

11:30—lunch

12:00—shop for clothes

2:30—chores

3:30—baby-sit

6:00—picnic supper

8:00—watch wrestling on TV

9:00—homework

10:30—shower and sleep

Around the World 32

I. c	2. i
3. l	4. f
5. h	6. e
7. j	8. d
9. g	10. a
11. b	12. k

Can You Tell? 33

I. C, E	7. C, E
2. E, C	8. E, C
3. C, E	9. E, C
4. C, E	10. C, E
5. E, C	11. E, C
6. C, E	12. C, E

Let's Get Lyrical 34

1. 'Cuz You're My Lemon Custard

2. If You Needle Me No More

3. 'Cuz a Frog Got into the Radiator?

4. I Will Be Your Top Banana

5. I Will Never Leave This Town

6. You Got That Huge Mosquito Bite

7. Since She Scarfed Down All My Food

8. I've Been Living Nightmares

9. When You Ordered Toast and Jam

10. I've Been Feeling Pretty Crummy

11. Ever Since My Honey Said, "Shut Your Trap"

12. I'll Buy You a Piano Grand

13. And I'll Be Your Heel Forever

Have I Got a Job for You 35

Tad: 2, 5	Blanche: 3, 4
Anselm: 2, 3	Zoe: 1
Perry: 3	

A Midsummer's Day Cream 36

I. a	2. c
3. b	

Pandas 37

I. a	2. c
3. d	4. b
5. e	

Ancient Farming 38–39

1. It was the only way they could get food.

2. The ashes from the burn fertilized the soil.

3. The mud from the bottom of the lake was very fertile and rich.

4. Terraces helped reduce erosion.

5. Answers will vary.

Sell It! 40

1. They want people to associate wealth and good living with their soda.

2. a, c

3. Answers will vary.

The Dust Bowl 41

1. Settlers over used the grasslands.

2. The soil was no good, and the region was dry and dusty.

3. They planted trees to break the strong winds.

4. The ridges trap water and help the fields grow.

5. Answers will vary.

Today's News 42–43

Possible answers include:

Tornado: High winds caused many buildings to blow down. Rushing water over a bridge caused a traffic backup. Lots of damage will cost the town a large amount of money.

Looters: Because of a broken window, the department store was robbed. Gusting winds caused a freezer door to blow off.

Picnic: The tornado caused the postponement of the picnic. A new date will be set when the reconstruction timetable has been set.

A Native Tale 44–45

1. Answers will vary.

2. She is taken away to attend school.

3. She wants to meet her penpal and experience modern life.

4. Her husband is mean.

5. She realizes they will be all right without her.

6. She is disappointed with him because he no longer embraces the old ways that he taught her to believe.